GW01418874

ISBN 978-1-331-04018-7
PIBN 10137031

This book is a reproduction of an important historical work. Forgotten Books uses
state-of-the-art technology to digitally reconstruct the work, preserving the original format
whilst repairing imperfections present in the aged copy. In rare cases, an imperfection in
the original, such as a blemish or missing page, may be replicated in our edition. We do,
however, repair the vast majority of imperfections successfully; any imperfections that
remain are intentionally left to preserve the state of such historical works.

1 MONTH OF
FREE
READING

at

www.ForgottenBooks.com

By purchasing this book you are eligible for one month membership to ForgottenBooks.com, giving you unlimited access to our entire collection of over 1,000,000 titles via our web site and mobile apps.

To claim your free month visit:
www.forgottenbooks.com/free137031

English
Français
Deutsche
Italiano
Español
Português

www.forgottenbooks.com

Mythology Photography **Fiction**
Fishing Christianity **Art** Cooking
Essays Buddhism Freemasonry
Medicine **Biology** Music **Ancient
Egypt** Evolution Carpentry Physics
Dance Geology **Mathematics** Fitness
Shakespeare **Folklore** Yoga Marketing
Confidence Immortality Biographies
Poetry **Psychology** Witchcraft
Electronics Chemistry History **Law**
Accounting **Philosophy** Anthropology
Alchemy Drama Quantum Mechanics
Atheism Sexual Health **Ancient History**
Entrepreneurship Languages Sport
Paleontology Needlework Islam
Metaphysics Investment Archaeology
Parenting Statistics Criminology
Motivational

ENGLISH · CLASSIC · SERIES

WITH · EXPLANATORY · NOTES

THE TASK

BOOK II.

BY

WILLIAM COWPER.

NEW YORK.

ENGLISH CLASSIC SERIES—No. 89.

THE TASK.

Book II.—THE TIME-PIECE.

ALSO INCLUDING, IN PART,

Book VI.—THE WINTER WALK AT NOON.

BY

WILLIAM COWPER.

With Introductory and Explanatory Notes.

NEW YORK:

EFFINGHAM MAYNARD & CO., PUBLISHERS,
771 BROADWAY AND 67 & 69 NINTH STREET.

A Complete Course in the Study of English.

Spelling, Language, Grammar, Composition, Literature.

Reed's Word Lessons—A Complete Speller.
Reed & Kellogg's Graded Lessons in English.
Reed & Kellogg's Higher Lessons in English.
Kellogg's Text-Book on Rhetoric.
Kellogg's Text-Book on English Literature.

In the preparation of this series the authors have had one object clearly in view—to so develop the study of the English language as to present a complete, progressive course, from the Spelling-Book to the study of English Literature. The troublesome contradictions which arise in using books arranged by different authors on these subjects, and which require much time for explanation in the school-room, will be avoided by the use of the above "Complete Course."

Teachers are earnestly invited to examine these books.

Effingham Maynard & Co., Publishers,

771 Broadway, New York.

INTRODUCTION.

WILLIAM COWPER, born in 1731, was the son of the Rev. John Cowper, Rector of the parish of Great Berkhamstead, Hertfordshire; his mother was of the same family as the poet John Donne. The father, it would seem, exercised little influence upon his life ; the mother died when he was only six years old, and forty-seven years afterwards, on receiving her picture from a friend, he paid to her memory the tenderest tribute of affection to be found in literature.

Soon after this event he was sent to a boarding-school, where his life was made miserable by the cruel tyranny of his companions. At ten he entered Westminster School, and there spent seven years in comparative happiness. Though extremely sensitive and diffident, he became a good cricketer and foot-ball player, and acquired some fame as a scholar. Among his companions here were Churchill, the poet, and the celebrated Warren Hastings. At eighteen he was entered at the Middle Temple, but law-books had little attraction for him, and he spent the most of his time in mild dissipation ; enjoying the intimate friendship of Edward Thurlow, the future lord chancellor, and the delightful companionship of his two cousins, Theodora Cowper, whom he would have married but for the refusal of his uncle's consent, and Harriet, who in after years was the " Lady Hesketh" of his charming correspondence.

For several years Cowper led the life of a briefless barrister, viewing with increasing alarm the diminution of his slender patrimony. Gradually signs appeared of the malady that darkened his whole life, fits of depression and melancholy, which finally deepened into madness. In 1763 his uncle obtained for him an appointment to a clerk-

3

ship in the House of Lords ; but an examination was required at the bar of the House, and the strain upon his delicate nervous system involved in the preparation for this ordeal resulted in insanity and an attempt to commit suicide. He was partially restored by tender treatment in an asylum at St. Albans, but his intellectual powers seemed now to be hopelessly shattered, and he withdrew from active life,— " a stricken deer that left the herd." His relatives, securing to him a small annual allowance, provided the remedial seclusion of a country home. At first he settled at Huntingdon, in the family of the Rev Morley Unwin, whose wife was henceforth to be to him " as a mother." Upon the death of Mr. Unwin, in 1767, the family removed to Olney, which was the poet's home for nineteen years. Here he became a close friend and companion of the Rev. John Newton, whose rigid Calvinism and austere practices were undoubtedly injurious in their effects upon the poet's weak and susceptible nature. Several times the old malady returned, attended by fits of religious melancholy and despair.

Cowper's life at Olney must be read in the " Task," which is a poetical transcript of his daily thoughts and occupations, and in the " Letters," which are the most perfect specimens of epistolary composition that we possess. His natural temperament was bright and joyous, and the beauty and delight that he found in simple things constituted a new revelation in poetry. Though his thoughts, " for the most part," as he says, " are clad in sober livery," a light and wholesome humor always plays like gentle sunshine through the gloom that shadows his genius. " My gold-leaf is tarnished," he says, " by the vapors that are ever brooding over my mind." While " John Gilpin's Ride " is the jolliest poem in the language, " The Castaway " is the saddest. To understand his personality aright, one must read the exquisite prose descriptions of his daily companions, his tame hares and goldfinches, his garden with its beds of grass-pinks and mignonette, and his "workshop," the little greenhouse, trellised with myrtles and overhung with apple-blossoms; and above all, the woods and fields about Olney, and the "slow-winding Ouse," which furnished the many pictures that he loved so well and painted so beautifully in the "Task." In a letter he exclaims: "Oh, I could spend whole days and moonlight nights in feeding upon a lovely prospect ! My eyes drink the rivers as they flow."

Cowper tells us that he was "a dabbler in rhymes" at the age of fourteen. During his London residence he wrote occasional essays for periodicals and love poems for his cousin Theodora. In the first year at Olney he wrote, in conjunction with Newton, the "Olney Hymns," among which are the old favorites, "God moves in a mysterious way," "Oh, for a closer walk with God," and "There is a fountain filled with blood." But it was his protecting genius, Mrs. Unwin, who really introduced him to the world. Being urged by her to write, as a means of diverting his mind, and finding increasing delight in the new occupation, he produced "The Progress of Error," "Expostulation," "Retirèment," and other long didactic poems. These were published in 1782, but attracted little attention. But another valued friend, Lady Austin, introduced him to fame. She had already given him the story for "John Gilpin," and was begging him to attempt something really worthy of his genius in the blank verse of Milton, when one day he answered: "I will if you will give me a subject." "Oh, you can write on any subject," said she, "write upon this sofa." Hence arose the "Task," imposed by "the Fair," which began in mock heroics, and grew into a noble poem of six books that gave to the timid recluse of Olney the position of first poet of the century.

In 1786 Cowper removed to Weston, one mile from Olney, where he completed an excellent translation of Homer. His last years were filled with agony. Mrs.

Unwin died in 1796, after a long illness, through which he had attended her with loving devotion. The shock reduced him to a state of hopeless despondency, and three years and a half later he was buried by her side.

"Cowper, in many respects, is the Milton of private life."—*Sainte-Beuve.*

"We read Cowper, not for his passion or for his ideas, but for his love of nature and his faithful rendering of her beauty; for his truth of portraiture, for his humor, for his pathos; for the refined honesty of his style, for the melancholy interest of his life, and for the simplicity and the loveliness of his character."—*Ward's English Poets.*

"He has been called the best of our descriptive poets for every-day wear, the familiar companion of every quiet English household. But though the 'Task' is full of scenery, it is not purely, or even mainly, descriptive poetry. More than its rural character is its deep, tender, universal human-heartedness. Man and his interests are paramount, as paramount as in Pope or any other city poet. Only it is not the conventional, not the surface part of man, but that which is permanent in him and universal."—*Prof. J. C. Shairp.*

"He does not seem to dream that he is being listened to; he only speaks to himself. He does not dwell on his ideas, as the classical writers do, to set them in relief, and make them stand out by repetitions and antitheses; he marks his sensation, and that is all. Thought, which in others was congealed and rigid, becomes here mobile and fluent; the rectilinear verse grows flexible; the noble vocabulary widens its scope to let in vulgar words of conversation and life. At length, poetry has again become life-like; we no longer listen to words, but we feel emotions; it is no longer an author, but a man who speaks."—*Taine's English Literature.*

COWPER.

THE TASK. BOOK II.

THE TIME-PIECE.*

ARGUMENT.

REFLECTIONS suggested by the conclusion of the former book. Peace among the nations recommended, on the ground of their common fellowship in sorrow. Prodigies enumerated. Sicilian Earthquakes. Man rendered obnoxious to these calamities by sin. God the agent in them. The philosophy that stops at secondary causes reproved. Our own late miscarriages accounted for. Satirical notice taken of our trips to Fontainebleau. But the pulpit, not satire, the proper engine of reformation. The Reverend Advertiser of engraved sermons. Petit-maitre parson. The good preacher. Picture of a theatrical clerical coxcomb. Story-tellers and jesters in the pulpit reproved. Apostrophe to popular applause Retailers of ancient philosophy expostulated with. Sum of the whole matter. Effects of sacerdotal mismanagement on the laity. Their folly and extravagance. The mischiefs of profusion. Profusion itself, with all its consequent evils, ascribed, as to its principal cause, to the want of discipline in the universities.

O FOR a lodge in some vast wilderness,

Some boundless contiguity of shade,

Where rumor of oppression and deceit,

Of unsuccessful or successful war,

Might never reach me more.   My ear is pained,   5

---

* The idea of the title is more simply expressed by the phrase "Signs of the Times." In a letter to his friend Newton, Cowper explains it thus: "The book to which it belongs is intended to strike the hour that gives notice of approaching judgment."

1. Compare Jeremiah ix. 2.

2. This fine imitative line recalls Shakespeare's "multitudinous sea incarnadine." Such effects can only be produced by aid of the polysyllabled Latin. The skillful adaptation of language and rhythm to the loftiness of thought, in this noble introduction, is especially noteworthy.

My soul is sick with every day's report
Of wrong and outrage with which earth is filled.
There is no flesh in man's obdurate heart,
It does not feel for man.   The natural bond
Of brotherhood is severed as the flax,   10
That falls asunder at the touch of fire.
He finds his fellow guilty of a skin
Not colored like his own, and having power
To enforce the wrong, for such a worthy cause
Dooms and devotes him as his lawful prey.   15
Lands intersected by a narrow frith
Abhor each other.   Mountains interposed
Make enemies of nations who had else
Like kindred drops been mingled into one.
Thus man devotes his brother, and destroys;   20
And worse than all, and most to be deplored,
As human nature's broadest, foulest blot,
Chains him, and tasks him, and exacts his sweat
With stripes, that mercy, with a bleeding heart,
Weeps when she sees inflicted on a beast.   25
Then what is man?   And what man, seeing this
'And having human feelings, does not blush,
And hang his head, to think himself a man?
I would not have a slave to till my ground,
To carry me, to fan me while I sleep,   30
And tremble when I wake, for all the wealth
That sinews bought and sold have ever earned.
No: dear as freedom is, and in my heart's
Just estimation prized above all price,
I had much rather be myself the slave,   35

---

8. Compare Ezekiel xxxvi. 26.
15. **Devotes.**—Strictly, *to devote* is to consecrate as by a vow;
hence to sacrifice or to consign to some harm or evil.   So in l. 20.
35. Cowper was not afraid of the so-called solecism *had rather*,
which, in spite of the grammarians, has been "good English" since
Chaucer.

And wear the bonds, than fasten them on him.
We have no slaves at home:—then why abroad?
And they themselves once ferried o'er the wave
That parts us, are emancipate and loosed.
Slaves cannot breathe in England: if their lungs   40
Receive our air, that moment they are free;
They touch our country, and their shackles fall.
That's noble, and bespeaks a nation proud
And jealous of the blessing.   Spread it then
And let it circulate through every vein   45
Of all your empire; that where Britain's power
Is felt, mankind may feel her mercy too.

Sure there is need of social intercourse,
Benevolence, and peace, and mutual aid,
Between the nations, in a world that seems   50
To toll the death bell of its own decease,
And by the voice of all its elements
To preach the general doom.   When were the winds
Let slip with such a warrant to destroy?
When did the waves so haughtily o'erleap   55
Their ancient barriers, deluging the dry?
Fires from beneath, and meteors from above

---

36. Cowper expressed his horror of slavery in three short poems:
"The Negro's Complaint," "Pity for Poor Africans," and "The
Morning Dream."

40. The judicial decision that "slaves cannot breathe in England"
was given by Lord Mansfield, June 22, 1772, in the case of Somerset,
a slave turned adrift by his master on account of ill-health, who, on
restoration to health through the charity of Mr. Granville Sharp, suc-
cessfully resisted the attempt of his brutal owner to reclaim him.   In
1786, England was employing 130 slave-ships, carrying 42,000 slaves.
In 1787, the Society for the Suppression of the Slave Trade was
founded by Mr. Sharp, William Wilberforce, and others.   In 1807 the
slave trade was abolished by act of parliament.   Slavery itself was
abolished in the colonies in 1834, at a cost to the nation of twenty
million pounds.

53. **To preach the general doom.**—"Alluding to the late calam-
ities in Jamaica."—*Cowper's note.*   Violent and destructive hurri-
canes swept over Jamaica in the years 1780–86.

57. **Meteors from above.**—"August 18, 1783."—*Cowper's note.*
This meteor is thus described in Mason's *Notes:* "It consisted of two
brilliant balls of fire, of the apparent diameter of about two feet, side
by side, followed by a train of eight others of smaller dimensions.

Portentous, unexampled, unexplained,
Have kindled beacons in the skies ; and the old
And crazy earth has had her shaking fits   60
More frequent, and foregone her usual rest.
Is it a time to wrangle, when the props
And pillars of our planet seem to fail,
And Nature, with a dim and sickly eye,
To wait the close of all? But grant her end   65
More distant, and that prophecy demands
A longer respite, unaccomplished yet;
Still they are frowning signals, and bespeak
Displeasure in his breast who smites the earth
Or heals it, makes it languish or rejoice.   70'
And 'tis but seemly, that where all deserve
And stand exposed by common peccancy
To what no few have felt, there should be peace,
And brethren in calamity should love.

   Alas for Sicily! rude fragments now   75
Lie scattered where the shapely column stood.
Her palaces are dust. In all her streets
The voice of singing and the sprightly chord
Are silent. Revelry, and dance, and show,
Suffer a syncope and solemn pause,   80

The intervals between the balls were filled up by a luminous substance of irregular shape, and the whole was terminated by a blaze of light."

62. Compare Job ix. 6.

64. **And nature.**—"Alluding to the fog that covered both Europe and Asia during the whole summer of 1783."—*Cowper's note.*

68. **Frowning signals.**—Cowper expressed only the prevailing belief of the puritanism of his time in regarding the disturbances of nature as direct manifestations of God's wrath. Physical science had not yet cleared away the superstition that befogged even the most intelligent minds.

72. **Peccancy.**—Sinfulness; Lat. *peccare*, to sin. All are united by a common bond of sin. See l. 155.

75–132. The earthquake in Sicily here described occurred in 1782. Messina was utterly destroyed and the larger portion of the inhabitants perished, with them the aged prince who "with half his people" put to sea, hoping thus to escape.

78. Compare Isaiah xxiv. 8.

79. **Syncope.**—A medical term, used here with questionable taste; a fainting fit, hence any sudden pause or cessation.

While God performs, upon the trembling stage
Of his own works, his dreadful part alone.
How does the earth receive him?—with what signs
Of gratulation and delight, her king?
Pours she not all her choicest fruits abroad, 85
Her sweetest flowers, her aromatic gums,
Disclosing Paradise where'er he treads?
She quakes at his approach. Her hollow womb,
Conceiving thunders, through a thousand deeps
And fiery caverns, roars beneath his foot. 90
The hills move lightly, and the mountains smoke,
For he has touched them. From the extremest point
Of elevation down into the abyss,
His wrath is busy, and his frown is felt.
The rocks fall headlong, and the valleys rise, 95
The rivers die into offensive pools,
And, charged with putrid verdure, breathe a gross
And mortal nuisance into all the air.
What solid was, by transformation strange,
Grows fluid; and the fixed and rooted earth, 100
Tormented into billows, heaves and swells,
Or with vortiginous and hideous whirl
Sucks down its prey insatiable. Immense
The tumult and the overthrow, the pangs
And agonies of human and of brute 105
Multitudes, fugitive on every side,
And fugitive in vain. The sylvan scene

91. "Bow thy heavens, O Lord, and come down; touch the mountains and they shall smoke."—*Psalm* cxliv. 5.
98. **Mortal.**—Causing death; as in "Winter's Tale," "This news is mortal to the queen," and in Milton's "mortal taste" of the forbidden fruit.
102. **Vortiginous.**—Like a vortex or whirlpool. Cowper was too fond of the *sesquipedalian* Latin.
107-110. "Near Laureana, in Calabria Ultra, a singular phenomenon had been produced: the surface of two whole tenements, with large olive and mulberry trees therein, situated in a valley perfectly level, had been detached by the earthquake and transplanted, the trees still remaining in their places, to the distance of a mile from their former situations."—*Letter of Sir Wm. Hamilton.*

Migrates uplifted : and, with all its soil,
Alighting in far distant fields, finds out
A new possessor, and survives the change.   110
Ocean has caught the frenzy, and, upwrought
To an enormous and o'erbearing height,
Not by a mighty wind, but by that voice
Which winds and waves obey, invades the shore
Resistless. Never such a sudden flood,   115
Upridged so high, and sent on such a charge,
Possessed an inland scene. Where now the throng
That pressed the beach, and, hasty to depart,
Looked to the sea for safety ? They are gone,
Gone with the refluent wave into the deep—   120
A prince with half his people ! Ancient towers,
And roofs embattled high, the gloomy scenes
Where beauty oft and lettered worth consume
Life in the unproductive shades of death,
Fall prone ; the pale inhabitants come forth,   125
And, happy in their unforeseen release ·
From all the rigors of restraint, enjoy
The terrors of the day that sets them free.
Who then that has thee, would not hold thee fast,
Freedom ? whom they that lose thee so regret,   130
That even a judgment, making way for thee,
Seems in their eyes a mercy for thy sake.
    Such evil Sin hath wrought, and such a flame
Kindled in Heaven, that it burns down to Earth,
And in the furious inquest that it makes   135
On God's behalf, lays waste his fairest works.
The very elements, though each be meant
The minister of man, to serve his wants,

---

114. Compare Matthew viii. 27.
    123. **Lettered worth.**—A good example is that of Silvio Pellico,
an Italian author and patriot, whose celebrated work " My Prisons"
(Le mie Prigioni) describes his fifteen years of suffering. Cf. also
Byron's " Prisoner of Chillon."
    135. **Inquest.**—Is this word well chosen? A judicial inquiry should
be calm, rather than " furious."

Conspire against him.   With his breath he draws
A plague into his blood ; and cannot use   140
Life's necessary means, but he must die.
Storms rise to o'erwhelm him ; or if stormy winds
Rise not, the waters of the deep shall rise,
And, needing none assistance of the storm,
Shall roll themselves ashore, and reach him there.   · 145
The earth shall shake him out of .all his holds,
Or make his house his grave ; nor so content,
Shall counterfeit the motions of the flood,
And drown him in her dry and dusty gulfs.
What then !—were they the wicked above all,   150
And we the righteous, whose fast anchored isle
Moved not, while theirs was rocked like a light skiff,
The sport of every wave ?   No : none are clear,
And none than we more guilty.   But where all
Stand chargeable with guilt, and to the shafts   ·   155
Of wrath obnoxious, God may choose his mark ;
May punish, if he please, the less, to warn
The more malignant.   If he spared not them,
Tremble and be amazed at thine escape,
Far guiltier England, lest he spare not thee ?   160
    Happy the man who sees a God employed
In all the good and ill that checker life !
Resolving all events, with their effects
And manifold results, into the will
And arbitration wise of the Supreme.   165
Did not his eye rule all things, and intend
The least of our concerns (since from the least
The greatest oft originate) ; could chance
Find place in his dominion, or dispose
One lawless particle to thwart his plan,   170
Then God might be surprised, and unforeseen

150. Compare Luke xiii. 4.
157. **The less.**—The less malignant. Force of the word *malignant*
here?
166. The doctrine of fore-ordination,

Contingence might alarm him, and disturb
The smooth and equal course of his affairs.
This truth Philosophy, though eagle-eyed
In nature's tendencies, oft overlooks ;   175
And, having found his instrument, forgets,
Or disregards, or more presumptuous still,
Denies the power that wields it.   God proclaims
His hot displeasure against foolish men
That live an atheist life ; involves the Heaven   180
In tempests ; quits his grasp upon the winds,
And gives them all their fury ; bids a plague
Kindle a fiery boil upon the skin,
And putrefy the breath of blooming Health.
He calls for Famine, and the meager fiend   185
Blows mildew from between his shriveled lips,
And taints the golden ear.   He springs his mines,
And desolates a nation at a blast.
Forth steps the spruce philosopher, and tells
Of homogeneal and discordant springs   190
And principles ; of causes, how they work
By necessary laws their sure effects ;
Of action and reaction.   He has found
The source of the discase, that nature feels,

---

176. So Bacon more clearly says : "A little philosophy inclineth man's mind to atheism; but depth in philosophy bringeth men's minds about to religion; for while the mind of man looketh upon second causes scattered, it may sometimes rest in them and go no further; but when it beholdeth the chain of them, confederate and linked together, it must needs fly to Providence and Deity."

178-188. A thoroughly Hebraic conception of a jealous and wrathful God who takes vengeance upon his enemies in this life. See ll. 155, 156.

181. Cowper is thinking, perhaps, of Æolus (in the Æneid) when in anger he let the winds out of the cave.

185. **Meager fiend.**—So Virgil has "malesuada fames," evil-persuading famine. Cf. Shelley's epithet for death, in "Adonais," "the Eternal Hunger."

187. **Golden ear.**—Heads of the ripening grain.

189-196. Though Cowper would doubtless speak more respectfully of modern science, yet his satire may be not inappropriately applied to the self-complacent assumption of omniscience displayed by many of its great representatives.

And bids the world take heart and banish fear. 195
Thou fool! Will thy discovery of the cause
Suspend the effect, or heal it? Has not God
Still wrought by means since first he made the world?
And did he not of old employ his means
To drown it? What is his creation less 200
Than a capacious reservoir of means
Formed for his use, and ready at his will?
Go, dress thine eye with eye-salve; ask of him,
Or ask of whomsoever he has taught,
And learn, though late, the genuine cause of all. 205
  England, with all thy faults, I love thee still—
My country! and while yet a nook is left
Where English minds and manners may be found,
Shall be constrained to love thee. Though thy clime
Be fickle, and thy year, most part, deformed 210
With dripping rains, or withered by a frost,
I would not yet exchange thy sullen skies,
And fields without a flower, for warmer France
With all her vines; nor for Ausonia's groves
Of golden fruitage, and her myrtle bowers. 215

---

196. Such methods of "suspending the effect" as vaccination, lightning-rods, weather-signals, etc., suggest the answer.
197–202. All second causes are but the means of expressing or asserting the first cause, God.
  In calling creation a "capacious reservoir" Cowper is even less poetical than philosophical.
206. So again in Bk. III.:
                    "In whom I see
    Much that I love, and more that I admire,
    And all that I abhor; thou freckled fair,
    That pleases and yet shocks me."

209. In Book V. he says:

    "My native nook of earth! thy clime is rude,
    Replete with vapors, and disposes much
    All hearts to sadness, and none more than mine."

214. **Ausonia.**—A poetical name for Italy. Cf. Campbell's "Gertrude of Wyoming," ii. 15:
                    "Romantic Spain,
    Gay lilied fields of France; or, more refined,
    The soft Ausonia's monumental reign."

To shake thy senate, and from heights sublime
Of patriot eloquence to flash down fire
Upon thy foes, was never meant my task ;
But I can feel thy fortunes, and partake
Thy joys and sorrows, with as true a heart   220
As any thunderer there.   And I can feel
Thy follies too ; and with a just disdain,
Frown at effeminates, whose very looks
Reflect dishonor on the land I love.
How, in the name of soldiership and sense,   225
Should England prosper, when such things, as smooth
And tender as a girl, all essenced o'er
With odors, and as profligate as sweet;
Who sell their laurel for a myrtle wreath,
And love when they should fight ; when such as these 230
Presume to lay their hands upon the ark
Of her magnificent and awful cause?
Time was when it was praise and boast enough
In every clime, and travel where we might,
That we were born her children.   Praise enough   235
To fill the ambition of a private man,
That Chatham's language was his mother tongue,
And Wolfe's great name compatriot with his own.

---

216. In "Paradise Regained," Milton speaks of the ancient orators
          " whose resistless eloquence
     Wielded at will that fierce democraty,
     Shook the arsenal, and *fulmined* over Greece."
221. Lord Chancellor Thurlow was nicknamed in Parliament the
"Thunderer."
221-232. Compare with this passage Hostpur's description of the
courtier at the battle, " I.   Henry IV." I. 3,—" a popinjay, perfumed
like a milliner," etc., etc.
227. **All-essenced o'er.**—Essenced all over.
229. The laurel was worn by conquerors, the myrtle was worn at
feasts.
231. Compare I Chronicles xiii. 9, 10.
237. **Chatham.**—William Pitt, Earl of Chatham (1708-1778).   "He
was admired by all Europe," says Macaulay.   "He was the first
Englishman of his time; and he made England the first country in
the world."
238. **Wolfe.**—General Wolfe, who died nobly while storming Que-
bec, Sept. 12, 1759.

Farewell those honors, and farewell with them
The hope of such hereafter ! They have fallen   240
Each in his field of glory ; one in arms,
And one in council—Wolfe upon the lap
Of smiling Victory that moment won,
And Chatham heart-sick of his country's shame !
They made us many soldiers. Chatham, still   245
Consulting England's happiness at home,
Secured it by an unforgiving frown,
If any wronged her. Wolfe, where'er he fought,
Put so much of his heart into his act,
That his example had a magnet's force,   250
And all were swift to follow whom all loved.
Those suns are set. Oh, rise some other such !
Or all that we have left is empty talk
Of old achievements, and despair of new.
Now hoist the sail, and let the streamers float   255
Upon the wanton breezes. Strew the deck
With lavender, and sprinkle liquid sweets,
That no rude savor maritime invade
The nose of nice nobility ! Breathe soft
Ye clarionets, and softer still ye flutes,   260
That winds and waters, lulled by magic sounds,
May bear us smoothly to the Gallic shore !
True, we have lost an empire—let it pass.
True, we may thank the perfidy of France,

242. **One in council.**—"Broken with age and disease, the Earl was borne to the House of Lords on the 7th of April, and uttered in a few broken words his protest against the proposal to surrender America. 'His Majesty,' he murmured, 'succeeded to an Empire as great in extent as its reputation was unsullied. Seventeen years ago this people was the terror of the world.' Then, falling back in a swoon, he was borne home to die."—*Green's Hist. of the Eng. People.*

263. **Let it pass.**—Impersonal *it.* Cf. "let that pass," l. 267.

264. **The perfidy of France.**—A treaty of alliance was made between France and the United States early in 1778, and a fleet of sixteen war-vessels sent, with 4000 men. Cornwallis surrendered to Washington and Lafayette at Yorktown, Oct. 19, 1781. In a letter to Newton, Cowper says: "France and, of course, Spain have acted a

That picked the jewel out of England's crown,   265
With all the cunning of an envious shrew.
And let that pass—'twas but a trick of state.
A brave man knows no malice, but at once
Forgets in peace the injuries of war,
And gives his direst foe a friend's embrace.   270
And, shamed as we have been, to the very beard
Braved and defied, and in our own sea proved
Too weak for those decisive blows that once
Ensured us mastery there, we yet retain
Some small pre-eminence ; we justly boast   275
At least superior jockeyship, and claim
The honors of the turf as all our own.
Go then, well worthy of the praise ye seek,
And show the shame, ye might conceal at home,
In foreign eyes !—Be grooms, and win the plate,   280
Where once your noble fathers won a crown !
'Tis generous to communicate your skill
To those that need it. Folly is soon learned,
And under such preceptors, who can fail !
   There is a pleasure in poetic pains   285

---

treacherous, a thievish part. They have stolen America from Eng-
land, and whether they are able to possess themselves of that jewel
or not hereafter, it was doubtless what they intended."

271. To "beard the lion " is a saying as old as the Greeks.

279. **Jockeyship.**—The name *jockey* was originally *Jackey*, di-
minutive of *Jack*, the common name, first of the groom, then of the
rider.

Cowper suggests ironically that it is some honor to England to
have been able to teach France the art of horse-racing.

280. **The plate.**—The prize of gold or silver plate, given at the
race, as the " Queen's plate."

280, 281. So Pope complained:

"The peers grew proud in horsemanship to excel,
   Newmarket's glory rose as Britain's fell."

284. See close of Bk. I. for a similar, though milder, outburst of
patriotic indignation at the folly of idle and effeminate Englishmen
who, " graced with a sword, and worthier of a fan," have made:

"Our arch of empire, steadfast but for you,
   A mutilated structure, soon to fall."

285. So Keats sang:

"Sweet are the pleasures that to verse belong,
   And doubly sweet a brotherhood of song."

Which only poets know. The shifts and turns,
The expedients and inventions multiform,
To which the mind resorts, in chase of terms
Though apt, yet coy, and difficult to win—
To arrest the fleeting images that fill   290
The mirror of the mind, and hold them fast,
And force them sit, till he has penciled off
A faithful likeness of the forms he views ;
Then to dispose his copies with such art
That each may find its most propitious light,   295
And shine by situation, hardly less
Than by the labor and the skill it cost ;
Are occupations of the poet's mind
So pleasing, and that steal away the thought
With such address from themes of sad import,   300
That, lost in his own musings, happy man !
He feels the anxieties of life, denied
Their wonted entertainment, all retire.
Such joys has he that sings. But ah ! not such,
Or seldom such, the hearers of his song.   305
Fastidious, or else listless, or perhaps
Aware of nothing arduous in a task
They never undertook, they little note
His dangers or escapes, and haply find
Their least amusement where he found the most.   310
But is amusement all ? Studious of song,
And yet ambitious not to sing in vain,
I would not trifle merely, though the world
Be loudest in their praise who do no more.

298–304. In a letter to Newton Cowper says: "Poetry, above all
things, is useful to me in this respect. While I am held in pursuit of
pretty images, or a pretty way of expressing them, I forget every-
thing that is irksome." In another letter he says: "Encompassed by
the midnight of absolute despair, and a thousand times filled with un-
speakable horror, I first commenced an author. Distress drove me
to it, and the impossibility of subsisting without some employment
still recommends it."

Yet what can satire, whether grave or gay? 315
It may correct a foible, may chastise
The freaks of fashion, regulate the dress,
Retrench a sword-blade, or displace a patch ;
But where are its sublimer trophies found?
What vice has it subdued? whose heart reclaimed 320
By rigor, or whom laughed into reform?
Alas! Leviathan is not so tamed ;
Laughed at, he laughs again ; and stricken hard,
Turns to the stroke his adamantine scales,
That fear no discipline of human hands. 325
The pulpit, therefore, (and I name it filled
With solemn awe, that bids me well beware
With what intent I touch that holy thing)—
The pulpit (when the satirist has at last,
Strutting and vaporing in an empty school, 330
Spent all his force and made no proselyte)—
I say the pulpit (in the sober use
Of its legitimate, peculiar powers)
Must stand acknowledged, while the world shall stand,
The most important and effectual guard, 335
Support, and ornament of Virtue's cause.
There stands the messenger of truth ; there stands

---

315. **Can.**—Used here nearly in its original sense, *to be able to do*, or *to have knowledge or skill* (A-S. *cunnan*; whence the Scotch *ken*, and the modern *cunning*), as in "King Lear," IV. 4:

> "What can man's wisdom
> In the restoring his bereaved sense?"

318. Swords were still worn by gentlemen in Cowper's day. The feminine craze for wearing "patches" or "beauty spots" on the face is best described in Addison's genial satire, especially in the essay on "Party Patches," *Spectator*, No. 81. In "Hudibras" Butler suggests one freak of the fashion in speaking of the

> "black patches that she wears,
> Cut into suns, and moons, and stars."

316–320. Cf. Pope's idea of the power of satire:

> "Yes, I am proud: I must be proud to see
> Men not afraid of God, afraid of me:
> Safe from the bar, the pulpit, and the throne,
> Yet touched and shamed by ridicule alone."

322. Compare Job xli.

The legate of the skies !—His theme divine,
His office sacred, his credentials clear.
By him the violated law speaks out   340
Its thunders ; and by him, in strains as sweet
As angels use, the Gospel whispers peace.
He establishes the strong, restores the weak,
Reclaims the wanderer, binds the broken heart,
And, armed himself in panoply complete   345 `
Of heavenly temper, furnishes with arms
Bright as his own, and trains, by every rule
Of holy discipline, to glorious war,
The sacramental host of God's elect !
Are all such teachers ?   Would to Heaven all were !   350
But hark—the doctor's voice !—fast wedged between
Two empirics he stands, and with swoln cheeks
Inspires the News, his trumpet.   Keener far
Than all invective is his bold harangue,
While through that public organ of report   355
He hails the clergy, and, defying shame,   .
Announces to the world his own and theirs.
He teaches those to read, whom schools dismissed,
And colleges, untaught ; sells accent, tone,
And emphasis in score, and gives to prayer   360
The *adagio* and *andante* it demands.
He grinds divinity of other days
Down into modern use ; transforms old print
To zigzag manuscript, and cheats the eyes

351–371. The picture of a certain Dr. John Trusler, doctor, book
seller, preacher, teacher of elocution, and literary hack. His spe-
ciality, apparently, was "coaching" ignorant clergymen.
353. **The News.**—Probably some newspaper in which the minis-
terial quack's advertisement appeared between those of two medi-
cal quacks, the "empirics."
360. **In score.**—A musical term: all the parts of a composition
arranged so as to meet the eye at once. He marks the sermons and
prayers so as to indicate the proper "accent, tone, and emphasis."
361. **Adagio and andante.**—Italian musical terms, *slow* and
moderately slow.
362. He touched up old sermons, printed them in "zigzag" type,
and sold them as "facsimile manuscript sermons." People in the
galleries looking down upon the pulpit would think them genuine.

Of gallery critics by a thousand arts.　　　　365
Are there who purchase of the doctor's ware ?
Oh, name it not in Gath !—it cannot be,
That grave and learned clerks should need such aid.
He doubtless is in sport, and, does but droll,
Assuming thus a rank unknown before—　　　370
‚G^rand caterer and dry-nurse of the church !
　I venerate the man whose heart is warm,
Whose hands are pure, whose doctrine and whose life,
Coincident, exhibit lucid proof
That he is honest in the sacred cause.　　　375
To such I render more than mere respect,
Whose actions say that they respect themselves.
But loose in morals, and in manners vain,
In conversation frivolous, in dress
Extreme, at once rapacious and profuse;　　　380
Frequent in park with lady at his side,
Ambling and prattling scandal as he goes;
But rare at home, and never at his books,
Or with his pen, save when he scrawls a card;
Constant at routs, familiar with a round　　　385
Of ladyships, a stranger to the poor;

367.　Compare II. Samuel i. 20.
368.　**Learned clerks.**—L. *clericus*, a priest; whence *clergy*. Orig-
inally any scholar, as in the Middle Ages all learned persons were
ecclesiastics,—like Chaucer's

　　　" Clerk of Oxenford also,
　　　　That unto logik hadde long i-go."

369.　**Droll.**—To jest or trifle.
378–394.　Cowper's denunciation of the clergy was amply deserved.
The historian Knight says: " The indecorum, if not the profligacy, of
a large number of the English clergy, for a period of half a century,
is exhibited by too many contemporary witnesses to be considered as
the exaggeration of novelists, satirical poets, travelers, and dissent-
ers "　Arthur Young said, in his " Travels in France," 1789: " The
French clergy preserved, what is not always preserved in England,
an exterior decency of behavior.　One did not find among them
poachers and fox-hunters, who, having spent the morning in scam-
pering after hounds, dedicate the evening to the bottle, and reel from
inebriety to the pulpit."　See Goldsmith's " Citizen of the World,"
Letter 58.
385.　**Rout.**—A crowd or rabble; in the last century, a fashionable
term for an evening reception.　See l. 629.

Ambitious of preferment for its gold,
And well-prepared, by ignorance and sloth,
By infidelity and love o' the world,
To make God's work a sinecure; a slave 390
To his own pleasures and his patron's pride;
From such apostles, O ye mitered heads,
Preserve the church! and lay not careless hands
On skulls that cannot teach, and will not learn.
    Would I describe a preacher, such as Paul, 395
Were he on earth, would hear, approve, and own,
Paul should himself direct me. I would trace
His master-strokes, and draw from his design.
I would express him simple, grave, sincere;
In doctrine uncorrupt; in language plain, 400
And plain in manner; decent, solemn, chaste,
And natural in gesture; much impressed
Himself, as conscious of his awful charge,
And anxious mainly that the flock he feeds
May feel it too; affectionate in look, 405
And tender in address, as well becomes
A messenger of grace to guilty men.
Behold the picture!—Is it like?—Like whom?
The things that mount the rostrum with a skip,
And then skip down again; pronounce a text; 410
Cry—hem! and reading what they never wrote,
Just fifteen minutes, huddle up their work,
And with a well-bred whisper close the scene!
    In man or woman, but far most in man,
And most of all in man that ministers 415
And serves the altar, in my soul I loathe
All affectation. 'Tis my perfect scorn;
Object of my implacable disgust.
What!—will a man play tricks, will he indulge
A silly fond conceit of his fair form, 420

397–408. See I. Timothy iii. 1–11.
420. **Conceit of.**—Vanity on account of his fair form.

And just proportion, fashionable mien,
And pretty face, in presence of his God?
Or will he seek to dazzle me with tropes,
As with the diamond on his lily hand,
And play his brilliant parts before my eyes,   425
When I am hungry for the bread of life?
He mocks his Maker, prostitutes and shames
His noble office, and, instead of truth,
Displaying his own beauty, starves his flock.
Therefore avaunt all attitude, and stare,   430
And start theatric, practiced at the glass!
I seek divine simplicity in him
Who handles things divine; and all besides,
Though learned with labor, and though much admired
By curious eyes and judgments ill-informed,   435
To me is odious as the nasal twang
Heard at conventicle, where worthy men,
Misled by custom, strain celestial themes
Through the pressed nostril, spectacle bestrid.
Some, decent in demeanor while they preach,   440
That task performed, relapse into themselves,
And having spoken wisely, at the close
Grow wanton, and give proof to every eye,
Whoe'er was edified, themselves were not!
Forth comes the pocket mirror.—First we stroke   445
An eyebrow; next compose a straggling lock;
Then with an air most gracefully performed,
Fall back into our seat, extend an arm,
And lay it at its ease with gentle care,
With handkerchief in hand depending low: 450

---

423. **Tropes**.—Rhetorical figures.

436 **Nasal twang**.—A sanctimonious affectation, generally supposed to have originated with the Puritans. But Chaucer's Prioress sang the divine service—

        " Entuned in hire nose ful semely."

437. **Conventicle** was the name applied in contempt to any assembly of dissenters.

The better hand, more busy, gives the nose
Its bergamot, or aids the indebted eye
With opera-glass, to watch the moving scene,
And recognize the slow-retiring fair.—
Now this is fulsome, and offends me more   455
That in a churchman slovenly neglect
And rustic coarseness would.   A heavenly mind
May be indifferent to her house of clay,
And slight the hovel as beneath her care ;
But how a body so fantastic, trim,   460
And quaint, in its deportment and attire,
Can lodge a heavenly mind—demands a doubt.
   He that negotiates between God and man,
As God's ambassador, the grand concerns
Of judgment and of mercy, should beware   465
Of lightness in his speech.   'Tis pitiful
To court a grin, when you should woo a soul ;
To break a jest, when pity would inspire
Pathetic exhortation ; and to address
The skittish fancy with facetious tales,   470
When sent with God's commission to the heart.
So did not Paul.   Direct me to a quip
Or merry turn in all he ever wrote,
And I consent you take it for your text,
Your only one, till sides and benches fail.   475
No : he was serious in a serious cause,
And understood too well the weighty terms
That he had taken in charge.   He would not stoop

---

451. Which is the " better hand" ?
452. **Bergamot**.—A variety of snuff perfumed with bergamot.
458. Cf. Job iv. 19 and II. Corinthians v. 1.
463. **To break a jest.**—More commonly, *to crack a joke.*
472. **Quip.**—A smart turn, jest, or sarcasm; as in Milton's " L'Allegro" :
        "Quips, and cranks, and wanton wiles."
475. **Till sides and benches fail.**—Until the sides of those sitting
on the benches are worn out with laughter, would seem to be the
meaning.

To conquer those by jocular exploits,
Whom truth and soberness assailed in vain.   480
    O Popular Applause ! what heart of man
Is proof against thy sweet seducing charms ?
The wisest and the best feel urgent need
Of all their caution in thy gentlest gales ;
But swelled into a gust—who then, alas !   485
With all his canvas set, and inexpert,
And therefore heedless, can withstand thy power ?
Praise from the riveled lips of toothless, bald
Decrepitude, and in the looks of lean
And craving Poverty, and in the bow   490
Respectful of the smutched artificer,
Is oft too welcome, and may much disturb
The bias of the purpose.   How much more,
Poured forth by beauty splendid and polite,
In language soft as Adoration breathes?   495
Ah spare your idol ! think him human still ;
Charms he may have, but he has frailties too ;
Dote not too much, nor spoil what ye admire.
    All truth is from the sempiternal source
Of light divine.   But Egypt, Greece and Rome,   500
Drew from the stream below.   More favored we
Drink, when we choose it, at the fountain head.
To them it flowed much mingled and defiled
With hurtful error, prejudice, and dreams
Illusive of philosophy, so called,   505
But falsely.   Sages after sages strove
In vain to filter off a crystal draught
Pure from the lees, which often more enhanced
The thirst than slaked it, and not seldom bred

---

488. **Rivelled.**—Wrinkled, or shriveled.
491. **Smutched.**—Dirty, smirched.   Cf. "King John," IV. 2;
" Another lean unwashed artificer."
499. **Sempiternal.**—Eternal; from L. *semper*, always.
501. **Below.**—Away from the fountain-head.
505. Cf. I. Timothy vi. 20, and Colossians ii. 8.

Intoxication and delirium wild. 510
In vain they pushed inquiry to the birth
And spring time of the world ; asked, Whence is man ?
Why formed at all ? and wherefore as he is ?
Where must he find his Maker ? with what rites
Adore him ? Will he hear, accept, and bless ? 515
Or does he sit regardless of his works ?
Has man within him an immortal seed ?
Or does the tomb take all ? If he survive
His ashes, where ? and in what weal or woe ?
Knots worthy of solution, which alone 520
A deity could solve. Their answers, vague
And all at random, fabulous and dark,
Left them as dark themselves. Their rules of life,
Defective and unsanctioned, proved too weak
To bind the roving appetite, and lead 525
Blind nature to a God not yet revealed.
'Tis revelation satisfies all doubts,
Explains all mysteries, except her own,
And so illuminates the path of life,
That fools discover it, and stray no more. 530
Now tell me, dignified and sapient sir,
My man of morals, nurtured in the shades
Of Academus, is this false or true ?

---

516. In Bk. V. Cowper says we invent for ourselves—

" Gods such as guilt makes welcome, gods that sleep,
Or disregard our follies, or that sit
Amused spectators of this bustling stage."

517. Plato's answer to this question was not altogether " fabulous and dark."

526. **Nature.**—Man in his natural state.

527. With the change of times and beliefs, Tennyson's lines, in " In Memoriam," have come to be quite as true as Cowper's:

" There lives more faith in honest doubt,
Believe me, than in half the creeds."

530. " Wayfaring men, though fools, shall not err therein."— *Isaiah* xxxv. 8.

533. **Academus.**—The *Academia* was a public garden near Athens, presented to his fellow-citizens by Academus. Here Plato lectured; hence we have the " Platonic Academy."

Is Christ the abler teacher, or the schools?
If Christ, then why resort at every turn 535
To Athens or to Rome, for wisdom short
Of man's occasions, when in him reside
Grace, knowledge, comfort—an unfathomed store?
How oft, when Paul has served us with a text,
Has Epictetus, Plato, Tully, preached ! 540
Men that, if now alive, would sit content
And humble learners of a Saviour's worth,
Preach it who might.   Such was their love of truth,
Their thirst of knowledge, and their candor too !
  And thus it is.   The pastor, either vain 545
By nature, or by flattery made so, taught
To gaze at his own splendor, and to exalt
Absurdly, not his office, but himself ;
Or unenlightened, and too proud to learn;
Or vicious, and not therefore apt to teach; 550
Perverting often by the stress of lewd
And loose example, whom he should instruct;
Exposes, and holds up to broad disgrace
The noblest function, and discredits much
The brightest truths that man has ever seen. 555
For ghostly counsel, if it either fall
Below the exigence, or be not backed
With show of love, at least with hopeful proof
Of some sincerity on the giver's part;
Or be dishonored in the exterior form 560
And mode of its conveyance by such tricks
As move derision, or by foppish airs
And histrionic mummery, that let down
The pulpit to the level of the stage,

---

534. **Schools.**—Schools of ancient philosophy.
540. **Epictetus.**—A Stoic philosopher, made a slave at Rome in Nero's reign.   The " Enchiridion" containing his "Thoughts" is much admired for its pure and ennobling principles.
  Tully is the Roman orator and philosopher, Marcus Tullius Cicero,

Drops from the lips a disregarded thing. 565
The weak perhaps are moved, but are not taught,
While prejudice in men of stronger minds
Takes deeper root, confirmed by what they see.
A relaxation of religion's hold
Upon the roving and untutored heart— 570
Soon follows, and, the curb of conscience snapped,
The laity run wild. But do they now?
Note their extravagance, and be convinced.
  As nations, ignorant of God, contrive
A wooden one, so we, no longer taught 575
By monitors that mother church supplies,
Now make our own. Posterity will ask
(If e'er posterity see verse of mine)
Some fifty or a hundred lustrums hence,
What was a monitor in George's days? 580
My very gentle reader yet unborn,
Of whom I needs must augur better things,
Since Heaven would sure grow weary of a world
Productive only of a race like us,
A monitor is wood—plank shaven thin. 585
We wear it at our backs. There, closely braced
And neatly fitted, it compresses hard
The prominent and most unsightly bones,
And binds the shoulders flat. We prove its use
Sovereign and most effectual to secure 590
A form, not now gymnastic as of yore,
From rickets and distortion, else our lot.
But thus admonished, we can walk erect—

---

579. **Lustrum.**—A period of five years; so called from the Roman
custom of offering an expiatory sacrifice (L. *lustrum*) once in five
years for the purification of the whole people.
  580-595. **Monitor.**—More generally called "back-board." "A
careful and undeviating use of the *back-board*," says Thackeray,
"is recommended as necessary to the acquirement of that dignified
deportment and carriage so requisite for every young lady of fash-
ion."
  591. **Gymnastic.**—Athletic, vigorous; rarely used in this sense.
  592. **Rickets.**—A disease of the spine.

One proof at least of manhood ! while the friend
Sticks close, a Mentor worthy of his charge.   595
Our habits, costlier than Lucullus wore,
And by caprice as multiplied as his,
Just please us while the fashion is at full,
But change with every moon.   The sycophant
That waits to dress us, arbitrates their date;   600
Surveys his fair reversion with keen eye;
Finds one ill made, another obsolete;
This fits not nicely, that is ill conceived;
And making prize of all that he condemns,
With our expenditure defrays his own.   605
Variety 's the very spice of life,
That gives it all its flavor.   We have run
Through every change, that Fancy, at the loom
Exhausted, has had genius to supply;
And studious of mutation still, discard   610
A real elegance, a little used,
For monstrous novelty, and strange disguise.
We sacrifice to dress, till household joys
And comfort cease.   Dress drains our cellar dry,
And keeps our larder lean; puts out our fires,—   615
And introduces hunger, frost, and woe,
Where peace and hospitality might reign.
What man that lives, and that knows how to live,
Would fail to exhibit at the public shows
A form as splendid as the proudest there,   620
Though appetite raise outcries at the cost?
A man o' the town dines late, but soon enough

595-599. **Lucullus.**—A Roman nobleman, famous for his luxury
and liberality.   Horace tells the story (Epistles, Bk. I. 6) that Lucul-
lus being asked if he could furnish 100 chlamydes (mantles) for a
stage play, replied that he had 500 such "habits" at home which he
would furnish.
    600. **Arbitrates their date.**—Decides whether they are in fash-
ion or not.
    601. **Reversion.**—The property that is to *revert* to him when his
master is through with it; a legal term.
    608. **Fancy at the loom exhausted.**—Explain the line.

With reasonable forecast and dispatch,
To insure a side-box station at half-price.
You think, perhaps, so delicate his dress,   625
His daily fare as delicate.   Alas!
He picks clean teeth, and, busy as he seems
With an old tavern quill, is hungry yet!
The route is Folly's circle, which he draws
With magic wand.   So potent is the spell,   630
That none, decoyed into that fatal ring,
Unless by Heaven's peculiar grace, escape.
There we grow early gray, but never wise;
There form connections, but acquire no friend;
Solicit pleasure hopeless of success;   635
Waste youth in occupations only fit
For second childhood, and devote old age
To sports, which only childhood could excuse;
There they are happiest, who dissemble best
Their weariness; and they the most polite,   640
Who squander time and treasure with a smile,
Though at their own destruction.   She that asks
Her dear five hundred friends, contemns them all,
And hates their coming.   They (what can they less?)
Make just reprisals, and, with cringe and shrug,   645
And bow obsequious, hide their hate of her.
All catch the frenzy, downward from her Grace,
Whose flambeaux flash against the morning skies,
And gild our chamber ceilings as they pass,
To her, who, frugal only that her thrift   650
May feed excesses she can ill afford,
Is hackneyed home unlackeyed; who, in haste

---

624. **Side-box station.**—A place in one of the boxes at the theatre.

643. **Dear.**—The quotation-marks ("dear") must be understood.

648. Before the days of gas-lighted streets people who could afford it were attended by servants carrying *flambeaux*, or by "link-boys" with their pitch-and-tow links or torches.

652. **Hackneyed home.**—Driven home in a hackney coach, i. e. in a common hired vehicle, unattended.

Alighting, turns the key in her own door,
And, at the watchman's lantern borrowing light,
Finds a cold bed her only comfort left.   655
Wives beggar husbands, husbands starve their wives,
On Fortune's velvet altar offering up
Their last poor pittance.—Fortune, most severe
Of Goddesses yet known, and costlier far
Than all that held their routs in Juno's heaven !   660
So fare we in this prison-house the World;
And 'tis a fearful spectacle to see
So many maniacs dancing in their chains.
They gaze upon the links that hold them fast,
With eyes of anguish, execrate their lot,   665
Then shake them in despair, and dance again!
   Now basket up the family of plagues
That waste our vitals; peculation, sale
Of honor, perjury, corruption, frauds
By forgery, by subterfuge of law,   670
By tricks and lies as numerous and as keen   .
As the necessities their authors feel;
Then cast them, closely bundled, every brat
At the right door.   Profusion is the sire.
Profusion unrestrained, with all that's base   675
In character, has littered all the land,
And bred, within the memory of no few,
A priesthood, such as Baal's was of old,
A people, such as never was till now.

---

657. **Fortune's velvet altar.**—The gaming table. "The fine
gentlemen of the days of Chatham and Lord North," says Knight,
"pursued their vocation of gambling with the assiduous persever-
ance of the most money-getting tradesman."   Gibbon speaks of the
illustrious Charles J. Fox as having prepared himself for opposing a
certain petition of the clergy " by passing twenty-four hours in the
pious exercise of hazard; his devotion only cost him about five hun-
dred pounds an hour—in all, eleven thousand pounds."
661. Cf. Wordsworth's "Intimations of Immortality :"

"Shades of the prison-house begin to close
Upon the growing boy,
But he beholds the light, and whence it flows,
He sees it in his joy."

It is a hungry vice:—it eats up all   680
That gives society its beauty, strength,
Convenience, and security, and use ;
Makes men mere vermin, worthy to be trapped
And gibbeted, as fast as catchpole claws
Can seize the slippery prey; unties the knot   685
Of Union, and converts the sacred band,
That holds mankind together, to a scourge.
Profusion, deluging a state with lusts
Of grossest nature and of worst effects,
Prepares it for its ruin; hardens, blinds,   690
And warps the consciences of public men,
Till they can laugh at Virtue, mock the fools
That trust them, and in the end disclose a face
That would have shocked Credulity herself,
Unmasked, vouchsafing this their sole excuse—   695
Since all alike are selfish, why not they?
This does Profusion, and the accursed cause
Of such deep mischief has itself a cause.

   In colleges and halls in ancient days,
When learning, virtue, piety, and truth   700
Were precious, and inculcated with care,
There dwelt a sage called Discipline. His head
Not yet by time completely silvered o'er,
Bespoke him past the bounds of freakish youth,
But strong for service still, and unimpaired.   705
His eye was meek and gentle, and a smile
Played on his lips; and in his speech was heard
Paternal sweetness, dignity, and love.
The occupation dearest to his heart
Was to encourage goodness. He would stroke   710

---

684. **Catchpole.**—"An instrument formerly used for seizing and
securing a man who would otherwise be out of reach. It was carried
by foot-soldiers in combats with horsemen, and later by civil officers
in apprehending criminals. The head, made of light metal bars,
was provided with strong springs, so arranged as to hold firmly any-
thing, as the neck or a limb of one pursued, over which it was
forced."—*Century Dictionary.*

The head of modest and ingenuous worth
That blushed at its own praise; and press the youth
Close to his side that pleased him.　Learning grew
Beneath his care, a thriving vigorous plant;
The mind was well informed, the passions held　　　　715
Subordinate, and diligence was choice.
If e'er it chanced, as sometimes chance it must,
That one among so many overleaped
The limits of control, his gentle eye
Grew stern, and darted a severe rebuke;　　　　　　720
His frown was full of terror, and his voice
Shook the delinquent with such fits of awe,
As left him not, till penitence had won
Lost favor back again, and closed the breach.
But Discipline, a faithful servant long,　　　　　　725
Declined at length into the vale of years;
A palsy struck his arm; his sparkling eye
Was quenched in rheums of age; his voice, unstrung,
Grew tremulous, and moved derision more
Than reverence in perverse, rebellious youth.　　　　730
So colleges and halls neglected much
Their good old friend; and Discipline at length,
O'erlooked and unemployed, fell sick and died.
Then Study languished, Emulation slept,
And Virtue fled.　The schools became a scene　　　　735
Of solemn farce, where Ignorance in stilts,
His cap well lined with logic not his own,
With parrot tongue performed the scholar's part,
Proceeding soon a graduated dunce.

---

716. Diligence was freely chosen.
736. The Rev. V. Knox, a Fellow at Oxford, describes the " farce "
of a degree examination thus :　" The greatest dunce gets his *testi-
monium* signed with as much care and credit as the first genius. . . .
The examiners and candidates often converse on the last drinking
bout, or read the newspaper or a novel, or divert themselves as well
as they can in any way, till the clock strikes eleven, when all parties
descend, and the *testimonium* is signed by the masters." See
Knight's " Popular History," vol. vii. p. 111.
739. **Proceeding.**—Proceeding to a degree was a university phrase
for taking a degree.

Then compromise had place, and scrutiny 740
Became stone blind; precedence went in truck,
And he was competent whose purse was so.
A dissolution of all bonds ensued;
The curbs invented for the mulish mouth
Of headstrong youth were broken; bars and bolts 745
Grew rusty by disuse; and massy gates
Forgot their office, opening with a touch;
Till gowns at length are found mere masquerade,
The tasseled cap and the spruce band a jest,
A mockery of the world! What need of these 750
For gamesters, jockeys, brothelers impure,
Spendthrifts, and booted sportsmen, oftener seen
With belted waist and pointers at their heels,
Than in the bounds of duty? What was learned,
If aught was learned in childhood, is forgot; 755
And such expense as pinches parents blue,
And mortifies the liberal hand of love,
Is squandered in pursuit of idle sports
And vicious pleasures; buys the boy a name,
That sits a stigma on his father's house, 760
And cleaves through life inseparably close
To him that wears it. What can after-games
Of riper joys, and commerce with the world,
The lewd vain world that must receive him soon,
Add to such erudition, thus acquired, 765
Where science and where virtue are professed ?
They may confirm his habits, rivet fast
His folly, but to spoil him is a task,
That bids defiance to the united powers
Of fashion, dissipation, taverns, stews. 770

---

741. **Precedence went in truck.**—Position and honors were bought and sold, as by exchange or barter. Cf. Burke's speech on "Conciliation with America": "Despotism itself is obliged to *truck* and huckster."

770. Wilberforce thus describes his experience on first entering Cambridge in 1776: "I was introduced, on the very first night of my

Now blāme we most the nurslings, or the nurse ?
The children crooked, and twisted, and deformed,
Through want of care; or her whose winking eye,
And slumbering oscitancy mars the brood ?
The nurse, no doubt. Regardless of her charge,   775
She needs herself correction; needs to learn,
That it is dangerous sporting with the world,
With things so sacred as the nation's trust,
The nurture of her youth, her dearest pledge.

All are not such. I had a brother once—   780
Peace to the memory of a man of worth,
A man of letters, and of manners too !
Of manners sweet as Virtue always wears,
When gay Good-nature dresses her in smiles.
He graced a college, in which order yet   785
Was sacred; and was honored, loved, and wept,
By more than one, themselves conspicuous there.
Some minds are tempered happily, and mixed
With such ingredients of good sense, and taste
Of what is excellent in man, they thirst   790
With such a zeal to be what they approve,
That no restraints can circumscribe them more
Than they themselves by choice, for wisdom's sake.
Nor can example hurt them: what they see
Of vice in others but enhancing more   795
The charms of virtue in their just esteem.
If such escape contagion, and emerge
Pure from so foul a pool to shine abroad,
And give the world their talents and themselves,

---

arrival, to as licentious a set of men as well can be conceived. They
drank hard, and their conversation was even worse than their lives;
often, indeed, I was horror-struck at their conduct."
   774. **Oscitancy.**—Sleepiness, yawning ; L. *oscitare*, to gape.
   780. The Rev. John Cowper, a Fellow of Corpus Christi College,
Cambridge, who died in 1770, and of whom the poet says : " He was
a man of a most candid and ingenuous spirit ; his temper remark-
ably sweet, and in his behavior to me he had always manifested an
uncommon affection."
   789. **Taste.**—Appreciation.

Small thanks to those whose negligence or sloth   800
Exposed their inexperience to the snare,
And left them to an undirected choice.
    See then the quiver broken and decayed,
In which are kept our arrows! Rusting there
In wild disorder, and unfit for use,   805
What wonder if, discharged into the world,
They shame their shooters with a random flight,
Their points obtuse, and feathers drunk with wine!
Well may the church wage unsuccessful war
With such artillery armed. Vice parries wide   810
The undreaded volley with a sword of straw,
And stands an impudent and fearless mark.
    Have we not tracked the felon home, and found
His birth-place and his dam? The country mourns,
Mourns because every plague that can infest   815
Society, and that saps and worms the base
Of the edifice that Policy has raised,
Swarms in all quarters: meets the eye, the ear,
And suffocates the breath at every turn.
Profusion breeds them; and the cause itself   820
Of that calamitous mischief has been found:
Found too where most offensive, in the skirts
Of the robed pedagogue! Else let the arraigned
Stand up unconscious, and refute the charge.
So when the Jewish leader stretched his arm,   825

---

803. **Quiver.**—The university. Compare Psalms cxxvii. 4, 5.

813. Have we not tracked this wide-spread vice to its proper source, the universities ? Cowper overlooked many other sources of the general corruption.

817. **Policy.**—Civil power, or government, which looks to the interests of society.

825. See Exodus viii. 2–14.

"I do not think that drinkers, gamesters, fornicators, lewd talkers, and profane jesters—men, in short, of no principles either religious or moral (and such, we know, are the majority of those sent out by the universities)—can be dishonored by a comparison with anything on this side of Erebus. I do not therefore repent of my frogs."— *Cowper's letter to Unwin.*

And waved his rod divine, a race obscene,
Spawned in the muddy beds of Nile, came forth,
Polluting Egypt: gardens, fields, and plains,
Were covered with the pest; the streets were filled;
The croaking nuisance lurked in every nook;　　　830
Nor palaces, nor even chambers, 'scaped;
And the land stank—so numerous was the fry.

———◆———

THE· WINTER WALK AT NOON.

(The Task.　Book VI.)

THERE is in souls a sympathy with sounds,
And as the mind is pitched the ear is pleased
With melting airs or martial, brisk or grave ;
Some chord in unison with what we hear
Is touched within us, and the heart replies.　　　5
How soft the music of those village bells,
Falling at intervals upon the ear
In cadence sweet, now dying all away,
Now pealing loud again, and louder still,
Clear and sonorous, as the gale comes on !　　　10
With easy force it opens all the cells
Where Memory slept.　Wherever I have heard
A kindred melody, the scene recurs,
And with it all its pleasures and its pains.
Such comprehensive views the spirit takes,　　　15
That in a few short moments I retrace
(As in a map the voyáger his course)
The windings of my way through many years.
Short as in retrospect the journey seems,

---

6. Cowper, while wandering about in his favorite fields, could hear
the bells of Olney and of the neighboring village of Emberton.

It seemed not always short; the rugged path,   20
And prospect of so dreary and forlorn,
Moved many a sigh at its disheartening length.
Yet feeling present evils, while the past
Faintly impress the mind, or not at all,
How readily we wish time spent revoked,   25
That we might try the ground again where once
(Through inexperience, as we now perceive),
We missed that happiness we might have found!
Some friend is gone, perhaps his son's best friend,
A father, whose authority, in show   30
When most severe, and mustering all its force,
Was but the graver countenance of love;
Whose favor, like the clouds of spring, might lower,
And utter now and then an awful voice,
But had a blessing in its darkest frown,   35
Threatening at once and nourishing the plant.
We loved, but not enough, the gentle hand
That reared us. At a thoughtless age, allured
By every gilded folly, we renounced
His sheltering side, and wilfully forewent   40
That converse, which we now in vain regret.
How gladly would the man recall to life
The boy's neglected sire! a mother too,
That softer friend, perhaps more gladly still,
Might he demand them at the gates of death.   45
Sorrow has, since they went, subdued and tamed
The playful humor; he could now endure
(Himself grown sober in the vale of tears),
And feel a parent's presence no restraint.

---

30. Compare " Paradise Lost," x. 1094:
    " In whose look serene,
When angry most he seemed and most severe,
What else but favor, grace, and mercy shone ?"

30–50. In this passage Cowper seems to be thinking of his own parents. His regard for his father was respect rather than love; his devoted love for his mother is most beautifully enshrined in the poem " On the Receipt of my Mother's Picture."

But not to understand a treasure's worth,   50
Till time has stolen away the slighted good,
Is cause of half the poverty we feel,
And makes the world the wilderness it is.
The few that pray at all pray oft amiss,
And seeking grace too improve the prize they hold,   55
Would urge a wiser suit than asking more.
  The night was winter in his roughest mood; ·
The morning sharp and clear.   But now at noon
Upon the southern side of the slant hills,
And where the woods fence off the northern blast,   60
The season smiles, resigning all its rage,
And has the warmth of May.   The vault is blue
Without a cloud, and white without a speck
The dazzling splendor of the scene below.
Again the harmony comes o'er the vale,   65
And through the trees I view the embattled tower
Whence all the music.   I again perceive
The soothing influence of the wafted strains,
And settle in soft musings as I tread
The walk, still verdant, under oaks and elms,   70
Whose outspread branches overarch the glade.
The roof, though movable through all its length
As the wind sways it, has yet well sufficed,
And, intercepting in their silent fall
The frequent flakes, has kept a path for me.   75
No noise is here, or none that hinders thought.
The redbreast warbles still, but is content

50–54. Cf. "All's Well that Ends Well," V. 3:—
             "Our rash faults
Make trivial price of what we have,
Not knowing them until we know their grave."
52. **Poverty.**—Spiritual poverty, isolation, want of friends.
70. This walk, "under oaks and elms," whence the battlemented
tower of Emberton church is visible, is in the park, described in Book
I., belonging to Mr. Throgmorton, the "Benevolus" who "spares me
yet These chestnuts ranged in corresponding lines." There are three
of these noble avenues in the park, whose "obsolete prolixity of
shade" is still carefully "reprieved" by the present owner.

With slender notes, and more than half suppressed ;
Pleased with his solitude, and flitting light
From spray to spray, where'er he rests he shakes   80
From many a twig the pendant drops of ice,
That tinkle in the withered leaves below.
Stillness, accompanied with sounds so soft,
Charms more than silence.   Meditation here
May think down hours to moments.   Here the heart   85
May give a useful lesson to the head,
And learning wiser grow without his books.
Knowledge and Wisdom, far from being one,
Have ofttimes no connection.   Knowledge dwells
In heads replete with thoughts of other men ;   90
Wisdom in minds attentive to their own.
Knowledge, a rude unprofitable mass,
The mere materials with which Wisdom builds,
Till smoothed, and squared, and fitted to its place,
Does but encumber whom it seems to enrich.   95
Knowledge is proud that he has learned so much ;
Wisdom is humble that he knows no more.
Books are not seldom talismans and spells,
By which the magic art of shrewder wits
Holds an unthinking multitude enthralled.   100
Some to the fascination of a name
Surrender judgment hoodwinked.   Some the style
Infatuates, and through labyrinths and wilds
Of error leads them, by a tune entranced.
While sloth seduces more, too weak to bear   105
The insupportable fatigue of thought,

100-104. Cf. Pope's " Essay on Criticism:"—
          " What woful stuff this madrigal would be,
          In some starved hackney sonneteer, or me!
          But let a lord once own the happy lines,
          How the wit brightens! how the style refines!"
And again: " Others for language all their care express,
          And value books, as women men, for dress;
          Their praise is still—The style is excellent!
          The sense, they humbly take upon content."

And swallowing therefore without pause or choice,
The total grist unsifted, husks and all.
But trees and rivulets, whose rapid course
Defies the check of winter, haunts of deer,　　　　110
And sheep-walks populous with bleating lambs,
And lanes in which the primrose ere her time
Peeps through the moss, that clothes the hawthorn root,
Deceive no student.　Wisdom there, and truth,
Not shy, as in the world, and to be won　　　　115
By slow solicitation, seize at once
The roving thought, and fix it on themselves.
　What prodigies can power divine perform
More grand than it produces year by year,
And all in sight of inattentive man?　　　　120
Familiar with the effect, we slight the cause,
And in the constancy of nature's course,
The regular return of genial months,
And renovation of a faded world,
See naught to wonder at.　Should God again,　　　　125
As once in Gibeon, interrupt the race
Of the undeviating and punctual sun,
How would the world admire!　But speaks it less
An agency divine, to make him know
His moment when to sink, and when to rise,　　　　130
Age after age, than to arrest his course?
All we behold is miracle; but seen
So duly, all is miracle in vain.
Where now the vital energy that moved,
While summer was, the pure and subtle lymph　　　　135
Through the imperceptible meandering veins
Of leaf and flower?　It sleeps; and the icy touch
Of unprolific winter has impressed

---

112. **The primrose ere her time.**—Milton's " rath primrose that forsaken dies," in " Lycidas."
126. Joshua x. 12-14.
127. Compare Psalm civ. 19,

A cold stagnation on the intestine tide.
But let the months go round, a few short months, 140
And all shall be restored.   These naked shoots,
Barren as lances, among which the wind
Makes wintry music, sighing as it goes,
Shall put their graceful foliage on again,
And more aspiring, and with ampler spread, 145
Shall boast new charms, and more than they have lost.
Then each in its peculiar honors clad,
Shall publish even to the distant eye,
Its family and tribe.   Laburnum, rich
In streaming gold ; syringa, ivory pure ; 150
The scentless and the scented rose, this red
And of an humbler growth, the other tall ;
And throwing up into the darkest gloom
Of neighboring cypress, or more sable yew,
Her silver globes, light as the foamy surf 155
That the wind severs from the broken wave ;
The lilac, various in array, now white,
Now sanguine, and her beauteous head now set
With purple spikes pyramidal, as if
Studious of ornament, yet unresolved 160
Which hue she most approved, she chose them all ;
Copious of flowers, the woodbine, pale and wan
But well compensating her sickly looks
With never-cloying odors, early and late ;
Hypericum all bloom, so thick a swarm 165
Of flowers like flies clothing her slender rods,
That scarce a leaf appears ; mezereon too,
Though leafless, well-attired, and thick beset,
With blushing wreaths, investing every spray ;
Althæa with the purple eye ; the broom, 170

---

139. **Intestine.**—Internal, inward; a questionable use of the word.
152. **The other.**—"The guelder rose."—*Cowper's note.*
165. **Hypericum.**—A species of St. John's wort.
167. **Mezereon.**—Spurge laurel.
170. **Althæa.**—Probably the marsh-mallow is meant.

Yellow and bright, as bullion unalloyed,
Her blossoms ; and luxuriant above all
The jasmine, throwing wide her elegant sweets,
The deep dark green of whose unvarnished leaf
Makes more conspicuous, and illumines more,   175
The bright profusions of her scattered stais.—
These have been, and these shall be, in their day;
And all this uniform uncolored scene
Shall be dismantled of its fleecy load
And flush into variety again.   180
From dearth to plenty, and from death to life.
Is Nature's progress, when she lectures man
In heavenly truth ; evincing, as she makes
The grand transition, that there lives and works
A soul in all things, and that soul is God.   185
The beauties of the wilderness are his,
That makes so gay the solitary place,
Where no eye sees them.   And the fairer forms,
That cultivation glories in, are his.
He sets the bright procession on its way,   190
And marshals all the order of the year ;
He marks the bounds which winter may not pass,
And blunts his pointed fury ; in its case,
Russet and rude, folds up the tender germ,
Uninjured, with inimitable art ;   195
And ere one flowery season fades and dies,
Designs the blooming wonders of the next,
        *   *   *   *   *   *

Here unmolested, through whatever sign
The sun proceeds, I wander.   Neither mist,
Nor freezing sky, nor sultry, checking me,   200
Nor stranger, intermeddling with my joy.

---

188. Compare Gray's " Elegy," St. 14:—
        " Full many a flower is born to blush unseen,
          And waste its sweetness on the desert air."
198. Whatever sign.—Sign of the Zodiac. That is, in all seasons,

Even in the spring and playtime of the year,
That calls the unwonted villager abroad
With all her little ones, a sportive train,
To gather king-cups in the yellow mead, 205
And prink their hair with daisies, or to pick
A cheap but wholesome salad from the brook,
These shades are all my own. The timorous hare,
Grown so familiar with her frequent quest,
Scarce shuns me; and the stock-dove unalarmed 210
Sits cooing in the pine-tree, nor suspends
His long love-ditty for my near approach.
Drawn from his refuge in some lonely elm,
That age or injury has hallowed deep
Where, on his bed of wool and matted leaves, 215
He has outslept the winter, ventures forth
To frisk awhile, and bask in the warm sun,
The squirrel, flippant, pert, and full of play;
He sees me, and at once, swift as a bird, 219
Ascends the neighboring beech; there whisks his brush,
And perks his ears, and stamps, and scolds aloud,
With all the prettiness of feigned alarm,
And anger insignificantly fierce.
    The heart is hard in nature and unfit
For human fellowship, as being void 225
Of sympathy, and therefore dead alike
To love and friendship both, that is not pleased
With sight of animals enjoying life,
Nor feels their happiness augment his own.
The bounding fawn, that darts across the glade, 230
When none pursues, through mere delight of heart,
And spirits buoyant with excess of glee;

---

205. **Kingcups.**—Marsh-marigolds.
224-229. Cowper says elsewhere:
    " I would not enter on my list of friends
    (Though graced with polished manners and fine sense,
    Yet wanting sensibility) the man
    Who needlessly sets foot upon a worm "

The horse as·wanton, and almost as fleet,
That skims the spacious meadow at full speed,
Then stops, and snorts, and throwing high his heels, 235
Starts to the voluntary race again ;
The very kine, that gambol at high noon,
The total herd receiving first from one,
That leads the dance, a summons to be gay,
Though wild their strange vagaries, and uncouth 240
Their efforts, yet resolved with one consent
To give such act and utterance as they may
To ecstasy too big to be suppressed—
These, and a thousand images of bliss,
With which kind Nature graces every scene, 245
Where cruel man defeats not her design,
Impart to the benevolent, who wish
All that are capable of pleasure pleased,
A far superior happiness to theirs,
The comfort of a reasonable joy. 250

ENGLISH CLASSIC SERIES,

FOR

asses in English Literature, Reading, Grammar, etc.

EDITED BY EMINENT ENGLISH AND AMERICAN SCHOLARS.

Each Volume contains a Sketch of the Author's Life, Prefatory and Explanatory Notes, etc., etc.

(Additional numbers on next page.)

ND - #0244 - 121222 - C0 - 229/152/3 - PB - 9781331040187 - Gloss Lamination